WHAT MAKES A MAMMAL?

THE ANIMAL KINGDOM

Lynn M. Stone

The Rourke Book Co., Inc.
Vero Beach, Florida 32964

PHOTO CREDITS
All photos © Lynn M. Stone

EDITORIAL SERVICES:
Penworthy Learning Systems

Library of Congress Cataloging-in-Publication Data

Stone, Lynn M.
    What Makes a Mammal? / by Lynn M. Stone.
      p. cm. — (The Animal Kingdom)
    Includes index
    Summary: Discusses the habits, bodies, and different kinds of
mammals and their relationships with people.
    ISBN 1-55916-195-7
    1. Mammals—Juvenile literature. [1. Mammals] I. Title II.
Series: Stone, Lynn M.   Animal Kingdom.
QL706.2.S76 1997
599—dc21   96–52189
                                                CIP
                                                AC

Printed in the USA

TABLE OF CONTENTS

MAMMALS

You are a mammal, as well as a human being.

Human beings are not the only mammals. Mammals form a whole group of **warm-blooded** (WARM BLUD ed) animals.

Mammals have hair or fur, and they produce milk for their young. Almost all mammals have four limbs—arms and legs or flippers—and give birth to live young.

Mammals are one of the **vertebrate** (VER tuh BRAYT) groups of animals. Vertebrates, including fish, amphibians, reptiles, birds, and mammals, have backbones.

Most mammals, including the giant panda here, wear coats of fur or hair. Baby whales have some hair but lose it as they grow up.

5

HABITS OF MAMMALS

Mammals hunt for food, eat, rest, sleep, and look for mates. Sometimes they fight. A few seem to play.

Certain kinds of mammals travel great distances to find new sources of food or shelter. These long journeys are called **migrations** (my GRAY shunz).

Mammals may live alone, like tigers, or in groups, like wolves and baboons.

A few mammals **hibernate** (HY ber nayt). They spend winter in a deep sleep. Brown bears and woodchucks are hibernators.

Hundreds of thousands of wildebeest migrate in Africa to find better pastures.

KINDS OF MAMMALS

Scientists separate the 4,000 kinds, or **species** (SPEE sheez), of mammals into 18 or 19 groups.

One group is made up of meat-eaters. Dogs, cats, otters, seals, and bears are some of them.

Rodents make up the largest group, nearly 1,800 kinds. Rodents have special teeth for gnawing. Rats, mice, squirrels, and beavers are rodents.

Bats are a large group of flying mammals. The three species of egg-laying mammals are in a group by themselves.

Koalas are marsupials. The young koala on its mother's back is too big for her pouch.

WHERE MAMMALS LIVE

Mammals can live in most kinds of surroundings, or **habitats** (HAB uh TATS). Whales, for example, and seals live in oceans. Many hoofed mammals, such as bison and zebras, live in grasslands. The lynx and pine squirrel love forests. Marmots live high on mountains, above the level of forest. Kangaroo mice live in deserts.

Several mammals live in homes they build. The beaver builds a dome house of mud and plants. Ground squirrels and badgers dig burrows.

The beaver builds a dome-shaped home next to a stream or lake.

Warm-blooded mammals, like this tobogganing tiger, can be active in cold weather as well as warm.

A young grizzly bear grows up under mom's watchful eyes.

BODIES OF MAMMALS

Mammal bodies range in size from the tiny hog-nosed bat to the blue whale. Fourteen hog-nosed bats weigh about one pound (457 grams). A blue whale may weigh 440,000 pounds (199,583 kilograms). That's the weight of about six million hog-nosed bats.

Bats have unusual bodies. The two front limbs are wings with tiny hands. Whale limbs are flippers, but they have leglike bones beneath the skin.

In deer, the outer layer of skin produces antlers.

Sea-going mammals have smooth, streamlined bodies with flippers.

AMAZING MAMMALS

The world of wild mammals is full of amazing creatures. The cheetah is so fast it can break most highway speed limits. Sea otters and chimpanzees use simple tools—rocks and sticks.

The elephant has a remarkable trunk. Zebras have candy cane stripes.

Marsupials (mahr SU pi ulz) tend their babies in pouches. The strange echidna and platypus are mammals that lay eggs.

The elephant seal makes one deep ocean dive after another, sometimes to almost a mile down!

The echidna is one of only three kinds of mammals that lay eggs.

PREDATOR AND PREY

Most kinds of mammals live on a diet of plants. Black bears and raccoons are among the mammals that eat a mixed diet of plants and animals.

Some small mammals live almost entirely on insects. Most bats, moles, and shrews are insect-eaters.

The big, meat-eating animals are **predators** (PRED uh terz). They hunt other animals, their **prey** (PRAY), for food.

The largest land predator is the Alaskan brown bear. It may weigh over 1,500 pounds (682 kilograms).

A Canada lynx hangs on to its favorite winter prey, a snowshoe hare.

BABY MAMMALS

Baby mammals may be helpless at birth or ready to run. Baby bears and opossums are both helpless and hairless. An elk calf, though, can run with its mother soon after birth.

Mammal babies grow at first by drinking their mother's milk. At least one parent guides them as they grow. A bear cub, for example, may spend three years or more at its mother's side.

Mammal mothers, like the sea otter, take care of their babies until they're old enough to care for themselves.

PEOPLE AND MAMMALS

Farm mammals are important to people. They are the source of milk, food, clothing, and companionship. Some farm animals perform work.

Wild mammals are important, too. They help keep the balance between predators and prey.

Some people enjoy hunting wild mammals. Even more people enjoy watching and studying them.

Wild mammals disappear when people destroy their habitats. Many mammals are **endangered** (en DAYN jerd), in danger of disappearing forever.

Glossary

endangered (en DAYN jerd) — in danger of no longer existing; very rare

habitat (HAB uh TAT) — the special kind of place where an animal lives, such as a cypress swamp

hibernate (HY ber nayt) — to enter into a deep winter sleep

marsupial (mahr SU pi ul) — a family of mammals in which the females raise their young in a pouch

migration (my GRAY shun)— travel to a distant place at the same time each year

predator (PRED uh ter) — an animal that hunts other animals for food

prey (PRAY) — an animal that is hunted by another animal for food

species (SPEE sheez) — within a group of closely related animals, one certain kind, such as an *elephant* seal

vertebrate (VER tuh BRAYT) — an animal with a backbone; a fish, amphibian, reptile, bird, or mammal

warm-blooded (WARM BLUD ed) — refers to birds and mammals, animals whose bodies keep a steady, warm temperature even in cold weather

INDEX